FEEL YOUR
WAY THROUGH

BALLANTINE

BOOKS

NEW YORK

Feel Your Way Through

A BOOK OF POETRY

Kelsea Ballerini

Published in the United States by Ballantine Books,
an imprint of Random House, a division of
Penguin Random House LLC, New York.

BALLANTINE and the HOUSE colophon are
registered trademarks of Penguin Random House LLC.

Hardback ISBN 978-0-593-49708-1
Ebook ISBN 978-0-593-49709-8

Printed in the United States of America
on acid-free paper

randomhousebooks.com

2 4 6 8 9 7 5 3 1

First Edition

Book design by Barbara M. Bachman

This book is for

MY HUSBAND, MORGAN.

MY MOM, CARLA.

MY BEST FRIEND, KELLY.

MY THERAPIST, BETH.

MY YOUNGER SELF, KELS.

THANK YOU FOR SPARKING

THE INSPIRATION THAT HAS

POURED INTO THESE PAGES.

MOSTLY, IT IS FOR YOU,

NEW AND OLD FRIENDS ALIKE.

I HOPE THIS BOOK DOES

YOU PROUD.

Contents

...

DEAR READER   *xi*

AUTHOR'S NOTE   *xiii*

I.

NEVER BURN THE BOOK   *3*

BECOMING BUTTERFLIES   *5*

DANDELION   *7*

YOU ARE WHERE YOU'RE FROM   *8*

YOU ARE THE SUN   *10*

HERE WITH YOU   *12*

II.

JUMBLED   *15*

THE SKY   *17*

LOOKING SIDEWAYS   *20*

ME AND PROMISES   *22*

WHEN IT RAINS   *23*

SPOTLIGHT   26

IF I HAD A SISTER   27

I ONCE HAD A FRIEND   30

FAILURE   32

RISE   33

HOLDING ME BACK   34

EDGES   36

III.

YOU'LL ALWAYS HAVE ME   41

KNOW IT ALL   43

THE CHEERLEADING TEAM   46

BEHIND THE MONKEYS   48

OCEAN   50

KANGAROO   53

HIS NAME WAS RYAN   59

SEXY   63

ROLE MODEL   67

THE RIGHT SIDE OF HISTORY   69

THE DRIVER   71

THE PEACEMAKER   74

IV.

LOVE IS   79

PERMANENT   81

THE LITTLE THINGS   82

MOVING DAY   84

SUNDAY DRIVE   86

ISN'T IT SAD   88

V.

GROWING   91

NOT MY AGE   96

MUSIC   99

NASHVILLE   101

FLATTERED   105

AESTHETICALLY PLEASING   106

PUT THE CAMERA DOWN   108

MOTHER EARTH   109

UNCOMFORTABLY ALONE   110

LEARNING TO LOVE ME   113

SHOWING UP   115

MY MOTHER   117

CHEERS   119

IF YOU'VE MADE IT THIS FAR   120

MORE THAN I NEED   121

A ROSE   122

ACKNOWLEDGMENTS   125

Dear Reader,

We're about to become close friends.

The pages to come unfold pieces of me I hold close to my heart. Abysmal insecurities, blissful epiphanies, hushed traumas, and hopeful dreamscapes.

Writing this book has been wildly therapeutic and has brought me immense joy. Thinking of you having it in your hands makes me want to explode with happiness.

I beg you to messy these pages. Take a Sharpie, highlighter, or paintbrush to it. Dog-ear, underline, scribble, and doodle as you go.

Rip a page out and tape it to your bathroom mirror. Get a little wine drunk with your best friend and stumble through it together. Share it with your daughter. Or your mother. Or a stranger.

Most important, feel your way through . . .

— Kelsea

Author's Note

Feel Your Way Through deals with themes of eating disorders and gun violence. These topics may be triggering for some, so please read with discretion. If you are experiencing trauma or PTSD, know you are not alone and please seek help.

I.

Never Burn the Book

. . .

our life is a story, albeit cliché
full of fairytale and fantasy hooks
firework feelings
turned burns beyond healing
but never burn the book

novelty moments all coming up roses
then the kings turn into the crooks
but there's healing in timing
so just keep on writing
and never burn the book

adventures abundant but stuck in redundant
small towns and homebody nooks
but now isn't later
there's much more blank paper
so never burn the book

all growing older and brushing less shoulders
with what-ifs of chances untook
the chapters seem sober

but the story's not over
so never burn the book

we can refont the title and repaint the cover
revise the way that it looks
but your life on these pages
is one for the ages
so never burn the book

Becoming Butterflies

. . .

growing, stretching, breaking
repeat, restart, repair
crawl out of patchwork skin
just need a little air

dusty attic boxes
the houses in our head
quilting disappointment
needle and a thread

discovering i'm sorry
giggles from the gut
chop hair off at the shoulders
escaping hometown ruts

crying on the highway
singing in the shower
blue jeans from consignment
cheeks painted in powder

wreck the car at sixteen
break his heart at twenty

gain a little weight
make a little money

in love with all the messes
waiting on tornadoes
pretending we have wings
wishing out from windows

impatient as the moon
changing over time
leaving our cocoons
becoming butterflies

Dandelion

. . .

like a dandelion can bloom
through a crack in granite

you can become something beautiful
wherever you're planted

You Are Where You're From

. . .

if you are where you're from
i am the mountains
white snow and cold rain
trickle down like a fountain
timeless and steady
offer views down to thousands
if you are where you're from
i am the mountains.

if you are where you're from
i am a slow drive
through middle of nowheres
wildflowers wide-eyed
getting lost is subjective
disobedient to time
if you are where you're from
i am a slow drive.

if you are where you're from
i'm a swing on a porch
weathered by wind
but sheltered from storms

a warm welcome home
before you get to the door
if you are where you're from
i am a swing on a porch.

i am a sunset, a small boat, a Kool-Aid on a blue float
the third pew, the kitchen, a Rocky Top religion
i'm ice cream, and football, meeting friends out at
        the west mall
i am free and i am love, if you are where you're from.

You Are the Sun

. . .

you are the sun
bright and reliable
people gather near your warmth
to grow, to soak it up

you often feel far away, out of touch
like you can never quite
get close enough
to the people that you love

but you think that while touching thousands.

without you, the world would be dark
you'd be missed.
paths would go untraveled
and skin would go unkissed

you burn at both ends
everbright, no doubt exhausted
but your fire isn't flawed
and there'd be a sad sky if you lost it

so shine like you have since the day
    you begun
and don't you forget, you are the sun.

Here with You

. . .

i swim in a bottomless
sea of what-ifs

an abyss to the brim
of possibilities

bathing in ideologies
flirting with mystery-lined plots

submerged in deep blue
of the haves and have-nots

but not a single one
of those hypotheticals
i've waded through
are as good
as right here.
right now.
with you.

II.

Jumbled

. . .

jumbled.
that's how i feel.
confused
messy
unhinged

nothing makes sense.
is it supposed to?
or is the whole point of life
to close your eyes
and feel your way through?

bumping into people
not knowing what's around the bend.
will the buildings shade the sidewalk
or will the sun burn through your skin?

i have moments of clarity.
some occasional confidence.
but they're hundred proof, neat
and i have a low tolerance.

so now i settle into the chaos.

see beauty when the castle inevitably crumbles.

feel comfort in not knowing.

find joy in being jumbled.

The Sky

. . .

the Sky watches the girl on the boat
proud of the way it cleaned up so nice
eager to impress with all its striking hues
not a cotton candy cloud in sight

the girl sits on the bow as the salt splashes her toes
but she's not looking out, instead down at her phone
so distracted she missed the dolphins that swam by
would have made her day had they caught her eye

the Sky watches
determined.

morning turns to afternoon
the ocean parades another blue
projecting onto the Sky like a feature film
but she's just hoping her drink won't spill

she's taking photos of the good time
she's not present enough to have
she'll then edit to make

the Sky more sapphire
and her eyes less sad

the Sky doesn't give up
relentless.

flaunting its God-given lure until
given the rightful attention
not holding over our heads
our eyes' lack of ascension

golds and fiery reds brushstroke the ocean's edge
as the afternoon gives way to the main event
a sunset too beautiful to believe
one if you blink you might miss

the girl on the boat looks up
at last seeing what has been so
steadily shining for her
she lays back while the rest of the world
becomes a blur

easing a smile, as if saying thank you
for patiently waiting with steadfast exert
the Sky goes cool and dark
resting, accomplished after another day's work.

Looking Sideways

. . .

i had to stop looking sideways, fearing another's stride
gaining strength and speed to a fictitious finish line

with focus elsewhere i missed my own victories
accidentally turning strangers to enemies

as i shift my eyes over my lane is degraded
slowing my stride and turning me jaded

letting what is, become reconsidered
creating a contest where no one's a winner

my feet like the asphalt, heavy and thick
realizing i will get nowhere like this

my eyes shift back quickly to a trail, mine to blaze
finally enjoying the ride, not the chase

sensing my maturity taking its own liberties
even feeling happy for other people's victories

because a win for someone else makes the bigger
    journey greater
and another's great success is not, in turn,
    my failure

Me and Promises

. . .

we have a lot in common
both know you top to bottom
slipping into the cracks in your foundation
wondering if we'll be forgotten.

close to the chest
your Achilles' heel
up your two sleeves
quiet, concealed.

but we're a package deal, they and i
loyal until our poets' words no longer rhyme
and as quick as we come, we say goodbye
in the instant that we catch you in a lie.

that's the thing about me and promises

you can't keep one without the other.

When It Rains

. . .

when it rains, i run outside
i don't reach for an umbrella
or find shelter to hide
i fling the door open
to confide with the sky.

lie flat on the ground
as it gathers around me
puddling up,
but i stay there soundly.
it floods the near garden
and drowns out the highway
my mascara has
slipped down my cheeks
running sideways.

but it doesn't matter
i can't hear the chatter
of the onlookers who must think
i'm a downright disaster
there on the asphalt

soaked to the bone
face to the sky
smiling alone.

it makes me wonder—

how often do our thoughts pass by
but we don't follow the whim?
how often do we want to see what's high
but don't go out on the limb?

caught up in worries of
who will think that we're weird
or the laundry list of things to do
there's no time to waste time here.

but what if we're really wasting time
doing all of the things that keep us
from laying down on a dirty driveway
or the grocery store parking lot
or the high school football field
and feeling the rain?

i zoom in.
it's cold, and it's invigorating
feeling the ground drinking below me
berating the sky on why it's taken so long.

i ask myself the same question.

Spotlight

. . .

every stage has a spotlight
the center of attention
making me feel bright
a daydream, a vision

stashing past-life skeletons
in shadows back behind
only playing up
the parts of me i like

when it comes alive
my pride holds its hand
feeding well my vanity
like only its glow can

every stage has a spotlight
that illuminates the heart
but oh, stages get lonely
when that spotlight goes dark

If I Had a Sister

. . .

if i had a sister
i wonder who i'd be
would my head have been held higher
entering elementary?

second-nature secret handshakes
tell and teach me about boys
shield me from the bitches
she knew i should avoid

i'd bounce off all my questions
on the messy parts of life
two bunk beds talking circles
straight through every night

i bet she'd roll her eyes
irately drag me to the parties
sharply hurt my feelings
but i'd know she was sorry

cabernet kept in the cupboard
but household rules defiant

she'd sneak a glass and subtly pass
to me so i could try it

i'd watch her hate her body
fight daily with her blue jeans
yell fuck you at the mirror
judging herself shrewdly

she'd bring home a new boyfriend
freshly manicured hands shaking
and i'd jump to dry her tears
if he left her heart breaking

we'd call each other nicknames
and every other in the book
but defend each other to the grave
if another wrongly looked

when mom and dad were fighting
as the knot began to fray
she'd swear we'd stick together
and that it would be okay

we'd go off to college
see each other every summer
we wouldn't talk as much
but we'd always have each other

i'd follow in her footsteps
walk the trail she's leaded
so one day our kids could have
each other just like we did

life would be so different
if the good and bad would run
in not just only mine
but someone else's blood

it's not that i feel lonely
ungrateful sad or bitter
i just wonder who i'd be
if i had a sister.

I Once Had a Friend

. . .

i once had a friend
who swore she had none

somberly saying "lonely is a cancer"
but when i'd call, she'd never answer

like she found comfort in
being unlovable
when really being loved just
makes her uncomfortable

emotional Plexiglas
built sky-high around her
but cool girl acquaintances
always surround her

spectators gawk
charmed in an instant
by her shadow-cast walk
and canyonesque distance

crying in glitter
blankets the floor
outsiders dance
in her disco decor

i hold hush stories
close to my heart
flattered she trusted
me with her art

for just a moment
i was convinced
our wine-washed talks
weren't only a trend

but just like the spring
sisterhoods end
two strangers again
i once had a friend

Failure

. . .

what if failure is only in the eye of the beholder
and i'm the only one capable of weighing down
    my shoulders?

what if i told myself that my so-called defeats
were only a different result than foreseen?

what if no one else saw my weaknesses like i do
and this sense of deficiency is only my point of view?

what if i took away the power from these thoughts
    and instead
rewired the pathways in my own head?

Rise

. . .

each time we fall
it is not the end
it is the beginning

for on the ground
bones and egos disheveled
we choose to level up
or choose to stay leveled

as time mends our skin
our hearts and our sores
scar tissue builds
stronger than before

gather pieces together
no time to blame life
this fall made you better
now it's time to rise.

Holding Me Back

. . .

infuriated when people don't text back
i scream
with thirteen unread on my screen

annoyed at stacks of dishes in the sink
i stew
while refusing to scrub them clean

hope to be higher
but not much of a climber

wish there was more time
but waste mine with wine

want the stars and the moon
but haven't made room

need the love and affection
i don't give my reflection

handfuls of excuses
gaslight my mind
my roots and my wings
have grown intertwined

realizing that maybe the
only thing holding me back
from who i want to be
is me.

Edges

. . .

i resent my softness
my Jell-O backbone
my squishy stomach

i wish my skin
would make a fist
and punch the air
exploding my
perspectives
daydreams
guts
everywhere

but i'm too scared

to speak up
to get it wrong
to piss you off
to be too strong
to be disliked
by anyone

pointed tongues
grace the stage
say what they mean
mean what they say

i try but it tastes like
lemon on my teeth
squeaky and sour
not for me

romanticizing rocks
thrown acutely at me
hoping they chip away
at my peacemaker cladding

roughen up my being
toughen up my backing
pop this bubble gum smile
till my fortress starts cracking

just wait,
one day i'll find my edges.

III.

You'll Always Have Me

. . .

thinking of my younger self breaks me like glass
things in her future, now things in my past
will sharpen her bones, and burden her back
i see her so clearly, but can't keep her from that.

she has bright turquoise eyes she gets from her father
a fawn-like waltz as her legs keep growing longer
she is eager and playful, unguarded and kind
i wish i could build her a fence to the sky.

she runs through sprinklers in front of the neighbors
strawberry popsicle smile, her favorite flavor
unbothered by her swimsuit and the way that it fits
a belly round with butterflies and Sunday morning grits.

she lives under a roof with her mom and her dad
two fish, one gerbil, three dogs, and a cat
a painted pink house in a small cul-de-sac
the neighborhood pool with a garden out back.

there are living room picnics, *American Idol* at seven
radio rides in the Jeep, Christmas ornament obsessions

the lights in the windows made it look picturesque
but there were three floors of dusty rugs unaddressed.

she thinks hometown is heaven, and the only place
    better is Disneyland.
she never wanted to be a princess, only wanted to bask
    in such beauty
to meet the women who defy the odds, holding birds in
    their hands
that ride off into the sunset at the end of the movie.

she loved to wear ruffles and dig in the dirt,
hair up in pigtails, one knee always hurt
neon imagination, small-town extrovert
only-child syndrome, a blessing and curse.

i wish i could slip her a letter.
tattoo it somewhere inside her skin
for only her to see.

i would keep it simple, short, and sweet.
it would read—
"you'll be okay, and you'll always have me"

Know It All

. . .

during my Girl Scout graduation from brownie
    to junior
our leader MaryAnn awarded each of her troopers
a word that embodied our personality
a turning of pages metaphoric formality.

i eagerly watched as my peers and friends
proudly walked over the makeshift-type bridge
awarded with words like "empathetic" or "reliable"
one got "loyal" another "excitable"
their cheeks blushed from the affirmation
while mine blushed from nerves of waiting.

finally, MaryAnn called my name.
my patent leather shoes made their way
over the bridge as she proudly proclaimed
the word she chose for me . . .

"informative"

i started my forehead elevens that day.
after years of field trips, campfires, Thin Mint escapades

collecting enough badges to cover my uniform overalls
she had labeled me
a know-it-all.

she was right.
i wanted to know
why the grass is green
why the sky is blue
every why, every how
to get to the truth.
i still do.

i am constantly reminded just how little i know
as i travel the world, oh the places you'll go
will make you feel small, selfish, and dumb
there's so much more than the town that you're from.

so many scenarios my head can't comprehend
the vastness of feelings deep under our skin
how they dictate our moods, our friends, our
    expressions.
how they change with disappointment, age, questions.

if we really understood the world and our ways
i wonder the level of pain we'd escape

the cancer we'd cure, the oceans we'd save
if we had all the answers tucked in our brains.

i now wear the informative badge with pride
as i pour out my questions eager, wide-eyed
taking in every detail, evermore enthralled
knowing no matter what, i will never know it all.

The Cheerleading Team

. . .

your name on a list is just letters on paper.

your feelings are vast
and feeling them's valid
but you have nothing to lose
if you're not on the ballot.

your insecurities ignited when you didn't make the team
but hindsight is, those girls were so mean
they would have crushed your spirit those Friday nights
in between screams of "go, win, fight!"

that was the year you picked up the guitar
it wasn't because you thought you'd go far
God knows you never thought you'd be a star
when every other weekend you had to switch cars
from mom then to dad, every time fall apart
catch your breath in a reality of three broken hearts
that you couldn't rebuild, only live amongst the parts.

you would have never heard the hum of the strings
you would have never known that you breathe to sing
you would have never realized your biggest dream
the day you didn't make the cheerleading team.

Behind the Monkeys

. . .

why first kisses are so hyped up
is still a mystery to me
mine was about as wild
as the place it was meant to be

already my friends had had their first kiss
joked and called me a late bloomer
but i was starry-eyed waiting for Chris
he was cool with a dry sense of humor

one weekend he invited me to the zoo
hinting *it* happening behind the monkeys
in the crawl space for kids to see better
i wish i was just being funny
but that's where this pedestaled first kiss
would play out if i was lucky

my friends gave me some preliminary tips
the main one being to wax my top lip
because the pre-teen peach fuzz would probably itch
so just pour some hot wax and one, two, three rip

i've never had the patience for "how to's" to learn
so that evening left me with two-degree burns
mom held back a laugh, said it wasn't that bad
and didn't let me wear makeup to cover the scabs

i was resilient and i am no flake
i put on a dress and went on the date
despite the oozing new look on my face
everything seemed to be going okay

we got to the monkeys
and then we kept walking
we got back to the entrance
and then we kept walking
we got to the cars
where our moms picked us up
he looked me in the eyes
slowly leaned in
and gave me . . .
a hug.

Ocean

. . .

i am scared of the ocean
maybe it's because i grew up entirely landlocked
where secrets of the water were a subject left untaught
other than my weekends at the neighborhood pool
with shallow-end gossip, lifeguards, and rules

littered with chlorine and spritzers half spilled
impressing our crushes with diving-board thrills
double-dog dares to touch the bottom at twelve feet
i never once worried while submerging that i'd sink

Norris Lake was my childhood ocean
really just an inland token
a few acres of muddy rain in East Tennessee
but when it's all you know, it's PCB

my family would go a few times a year
i'd jump out of the car, run down the wooden pier
ready to take turns playing captain with my father
pontoon somewhere with less people in the water
i'd inflate the floats till i was blue in the cheeks
cannonball, unbothered if the bottom brushed my feet

i'd swim and i'd kick
i'd splash as i'd drift
down the lake full of cheer
i never once felt fear

but, i'm scared of the ocean

i don't like the risk
the feeling of abyss
the mystery of what it is
and what it isn't

is she a woman, strong and serene?
or is he a man, mystic and mean?
does it depend on the day or the sun or the moon?
or the president or the trash that needs to be removed
that day? that week? that year?
where does it begin and where does it end?
and what do you *mean* we don't know how deep it is?

what if i tried to be friends and it didn't like me?
what would rejection from the ocean feel like?

knowing it could welcome me
or swallow me up whole
build a whitecap fortress
or bare its deepest soul

i thought it was irrational
but this fear i can't outgrow
so am i scared of the ocean
or am i scared of the unknown?

Kangaroo

. . .

i can't remember the exact moment i became aware of
    my body.

when the moments i used to spend daydreaming of what
    could be
turned to scanning for flaws, seen and unseen.

when afternoons spent making friends on the
    playground
became comparing my appearance to everyone around.

when Sunday morning blueberry waffles my mother
    made
went cold on my plate as i'd convincingly claim
i wasn't hungry.

a boy named Jackson called me "kangaroo" when i was
    a freshman in high school.
he was on the basketball team and i was categorically
    uncool

so you can imagine this comment made waves in my
     head.
he explained this new nickname because of my belly and
     little legs.

i had hated my body for years before that, i didn't need
     his help.
i certainly didn't need a team of the boys who only liked
     the cheerleaders calling me "kangaroo."
but they did anyway.

this coincided with my home becoming divided
couldn't help feeling like i was the only child slighted.
too much, too deep, too real to console
i began to flail in search of control.

i started taking diet pills
buying them like a pack of gum
insisting to the mirror it wasn't wrong
shuffling around my plate of crumbs.

there was a little less food with every little pill
hidden in the back of my bathroom cabinet

two an hour before every meal
my best kept secret, my worst kept habit.

after a few pounds gave way
to the caffeine in the pills
i decided that wasn't enough
i needed to steepen the hill.

so, i began bingeing and purging.
and that started working.

i'd make a generous order
consume the carbs i told my stomach it didn't deserve
excuse myself like a performer
lock the bathroom door and purge.

my five-foot-eight lanky frame
became a hundred and ten pounds.

my sickness told me i looked amazing
devouring the compliments like i should have devoured
    a meal.
addicted to the way the boys looked at me
and the way that made me feel.

i stopped trying to be invisible
and i started wearing heels.

but then i wanted more.

i got a membership to the YMCA
worked out a few times a week,
then a few times a day.

every second, every friendship, every good day,
    every party
was overtaken by my obsession with my body.

it took passing out,
privately, publicly, several times
then coating each one in embarrassed-soaked lies
swearing it's the summer heat or "forget about it,
    i'm fine"
for me to realize i had crossed the line.

my throat ached from the vomit
and my hands shook from the pills
my legs sore from the extra mile
i ran on the treadmill.

i stopped when i was eighteen.
the gym, the purging, the suppressants with caffeine.
i was starting to hate me
realizing those things would never make me happy.

i needed to show myself some accountability.
i needed to show my skin and bones some humility.
i wanted to get better, i wanted to start healing me.

my journey with my body has been littered with deceit
    and neglect:
sadly, several years of a lack of self-respect.
yet my body has kept me safe and healthy through it all.
never thought to quit on me, never saw itself as flawed.

it just patiently waited for my head to catch up.

what the world told me, and what it continues to
that women are not enough unless we are damn near
    see-through
that our worth lies in the gap between our thighs
or the structure of our face or the number called
    our size.

these lies we are fed are meant to keep us insecure, sad,
and small.
feeding us lies, while telling us to not feed ourselves
at all.
now it's bold and brave to stand in our skin so tall
and not pick up when projected insecurities start to call.

it is a process to find self-love.
it is ongoing and it is forever.
so if you're on that journey, know you're worthy
and we are in this together.

His Name Was Ryan

. . .

the morning was cold
i hadn't shaken the sleep from my eyes
the seventh day of sophomore year

my mother dropped me off
i slowly made my way inside
to the tangled teenage atmosphere

my low-rise jeans leaned against
the chipped paint on the cafeteria railing
encompassed in the copious Jake Hollister
cologne the jersey boys were spraying

the noise was sudden, loud, and sharp
the quickness, the panic made it hard
to get my bearings, but i was staring
at a boy with both hands to his heart

the hustle of the hallways
turned to a slow shutter speed
i was frozen where i was,
watching him begin to bleed

alarms rang out, signaling a lockdown
from a fellow Bobcat being shot down

my Spanish teacher was the closest authority
he sprinted to the boy, now seizing on the tiles
put his head in his lap, screaming urgently
get the paramedics dialed

after maybe one minute, maybe two, maybe five
i can't quite remember, i forgot all about the time
the burgundy pool around him widened on the floor
he wasn't moving anymore

the approaching sirens cut through my numbness
i wonder how many minutes i didn't blink
when i did, i realized most of the student body
were fight or flight, not freeze

there were only a few of us, with our delayed reactions
unsure if we were safe, convinced it was imagined

the classrooms were locked, eerily lifeless
lights were off, teens crouched on the sides

like drills we had practiced
played out in real life

one girl and i, soaked in our tears
ran with looped alarms piercing our ears
fighting locked doors lining the hallways
the mystery of who was knocking must have made
    them afraid

finally the art teacher opened a door
i fell inside, shaken to my core
i didn't know my heart could beat that quickly
worried it would combust within me

the alarms stopped ringing shortly after
letting us know we were safe from disaster

my flip phone clenched tightly in my hand
i called my parents, newly divorced
but in this moment unified
waiting at a nearby church

i went home safe
forever changed

His name was Ryan, and he died on the cafeteria floor
from a gunshot wound to the chest
i can't be too sure, but i think i saw him
breathe his last breath

we were both fifteen

that day, we went from strangers to lifelong friends
i think about him often, who he could have been

i'm scared of loud noises
i'm triggered by the news
i'm terrified of guns
i'm sensitive in crowds

but i'm alive

and because of a boy named Ryan
i know what a gift that is

Sexy

· · ·

we took a road trip to a city only a few hours away.
we planned to go to the aquarium with our afternoon
    to waste.

it was my first day free in months
exhausted but eager for some fun.

people didn't even know we were dating yet
our forbidden fling was my secret best kept
and our families would kill us if they knew we slept
in the same hotel room, let alone bed.

there was an unspoken curiosity in the car on the way.
raised up in church, i'd tried my best to wait
he had crossed that line before me
but i told him not to worry
that's all just yesterday.

we rented a room at the Holiday Inn
it was all that i could afford back then.
there was one bed, and in the back of my bullish head
i knew exactly the situation i was putting myself in.

the sky grew cold as the sun began setting
i felt my boundaries begin second-guessing
before i knew it, we were both undressing
in that moment . . . i stopped treading.

i laid down.
i closed my eyes.
i thought it was supposed to feel different.
i showered.
i got dressed.
i gave him my virginity.
and then we went to the aquarium.

. .

i was lucky enough to have the choice.
it is taken from so many
but even still, it leaves a void
i couldn't fill when i was twenty.

the thoughts of going straight to hell
were mixed up in a cocktail of
who can i even tell?
was i being safe enough?
and do i know if this is love?

i guess i should have known better
so am i stuck in this forever?
am i dirty? is he clean?
does this make me easy?

sex is messy.
and it isn't always sexy.

and that's why they say
don't jump before you're ready
but no one explained it to me like that
i cried for months, wishing i could take it back.

i wish for every person
every been there, every virgin
that if you are anything, be certain
and free of handsome diversions.

and if no one has told you yet—
you are okay.
you are not bad.
you are not broken.
you are not less
or somebody's token

or second-best
or forever frozen.
you are worthy.
you are whole.
and you can reclaim
your control.

it's meant to be beautiful, and one day it will be.
until then, give yourself the grace you deserve.
hug your body, quiet the thoughts
and don't ever question your worth.

sex is messy.
and it isn't always sexy.

Role Model

. . .

i was twenty years old backstage at a show
a mother in passing says "hey, you should know
my daughter is young now but as she grows
i'm so glad you are her role model"

at first i was pleased, like a dog with a treat
conditioned not only to want but to need
validation of my goodness, inject self-esteem
living to please as the role model

what i didn't realize, i was young at the time
and the title felt heavy, i didn't know why
but that was the moment i caged my own mind
to keep safe at all costs the role model

when life would get hard, i'd reach through the bars
he played with my heart like he played the guitar
i trusted too soon, now i have scars
that i cover up to be the role model

i woke up from my ego at age twenty-six
my cage was lonely with glamour and glitz

i looked through the iron, surprised, enlightened
seeing others removing their masks, unfrightened
i thought to myself will there be better timing?
do i finally let down the walls i've been climbing?

so now here it is, not filtered or fixed
i am not perfect, it doesn't exist
i am tattooed in flaws
i know them by name
even when shrouded
were far from erased
and if you think it's wrong
to walk tall in my shoes
and won't sing along
to those parts of me too
then maybe i'm not
the role model for you

The Right Side of History

. . .

did i misstep, did i misspeak
did i fuck up with that one tweet
i meant to raise my hand for the oppressed
voice the right side of history but instead
i am now misconstrued by both sides
from the unwritten words between the lines

that i should not have left unwritten
for people to interpret blanks left to fill in
because there was goodness in my intention
and now i can't begin to bear my mentions

it makes me want to shut up and sing
play a dumb blonde who stays squeaky clean
where my stage made of privilege is safe and serene
and in my cage made of complacency, people aren't
    mean

but i want to stay hungry and mindful and eager
always the student, never the teacher
an ally, a friend, the girl in the bleachers
screaming for the invisible "it's time to see her"

so, i'm going to let this one play out how it will
after all, if i am going to die on a hill
i'm glad it's for tarnishing a crown once so glittery
and trying to be on the right side of history.

The Driver

. . .

have you ever been cruising along in life
blissfully enjoying a freedom drive
then BAM, all of a sudden, you're the roadkill?

you were in your own lane, full of unfiltered wonder
and the next minute there's a bus that you're under

you tell yourself they didn't see you, it must've been a
    blind spot
maybe they were in a rush, that's why they didn't stop

"he seemed like the good kind"
or "she's my real friend"
your silver lining insists

you peel yourself up with much needing to be
    reconstructed
that'll take some time, as it was your feelings that were
    fucked with

luckily, second chances are in your nature, always
    offered out like candy
and your ability to erase the paper keeping tallies is
    uncanny

after your ego and heart repair, you make it back onto
    your road.
the high road. the one that assumes the best in people.
the one that assumes that "the more miles we travel,
    the better drivers we become
and the better drivers we become, the less we hit along
    the way."

you start again, hesitant but hopeful. slow but steady
    indeed
you want to enjoy the ride more than you've ever craved
    the speed
you start to feel the sun and the wind and the song as
    it spins
and right when you get comfortable . . . it happens again

BAM, roadkill.

can you call it coincidence if it happens twice?
you do anyway, removing the knife
not an ill word escapes your quivering lip
as unscathed they proceed, and you call it a slip

the pattern happens again. and again.

with every fluke, yours are lonely tears shed
with every deception, it's less highway you tread
the manipulation, infatuation, and bullshit loyalty
are all falsehoods you're fed, and i assure you it plays
not in theirs, but in your head.

so, i ask . . .
how many times will you get tangled in those tires
before you stop blaming the car,
and start blaming the driver?

The Peacemaker

. . .

you spend your childhood developing your personality
    type
i became a peacemaker

i developed the habit of throwing myself in front of cars
patching and piecing to mend strangers' hearts
juggling tears of bullies and jesters
taking back cheats, thinking they'd better

even with the purest intent i go out of my skin
to ask for a limb when i'm drowning
even with a knowing of self, i stay in my shell
when everyone around me is shouting

at my happy's expense i paint on a smile
perform until front rows are clapping
stay loyal to both faces of people
who cover their shit talk in trappings

i am no victim, i am a clown
all self-inflicted, amity endowed

you wish for new heights, i will lay down
but it is your choice to step on me when i do

you don't know me . . .
but do you like me?
you don't?
why?

just like that, i begin to cry
i guess i should change, so let me rearrange
the furniture in my apartment that i worked hard to
    pay for
i love it as is, but you probably won't
and after all, i did invite you into *my* home

i'll pour my best cabernet undermining the night away
but you'll go tell everyone i'm a fake girl either way
because you don't care to know me
you already decided you don't like me
and that is the deepest cut you can give someone
    like me

sure, it is a superpower
to care so deeply about others' happiness, health,
      energy, wealth
but it is also my deepest flaw, because i can never tell
how i am, where i'm at, if i'm doing well

most of the time, i am, thanks for asking

my Miss America answer will always be world peace
as i contort my bones to find it
Vaseline teeth rubber smile
bandage wounds of giants

as the planet spins
and we all hurt or get hurt by our neighbors,
i'm here for you, don't you cry
i am a peacemaker.

IV.

Love Is

. . .

the bravest thing you can be is yourself
in a world that hasn't caught up
standing in your truth, my dear
is standing in the sun

Love isn't anyone's to build a wall around
or give structure to
or create rules for
or judge when it looks different
than mine, than yours

if Hate truly is the greatest cancer
isn't it time we change the standard?
outdated, prejudice, small-minded slander
shut up and just let Love be the answer?

if acceptance can outgrow
just "a boy and a girl"
we would watch as like ivy
it covers our world

where every color of the rainbow
is celebrated like it should
where lovers aren't labeled
or misunderstood

the most magical feeling to ever exist
the most powerful emotion, a heart with a fist
the glance of a stranger, a comfortable kiss
a butterfly smile, a vow till the end

although it may only be found by the lucky some
Love is for everyone.

Permanent

. . .

you are etched into me
a carved heart on a tree
permanent.

you refuse a tattoo
i'm already on you
permanent.

memories in guitars
fingers overlaid in scars
permanent.

deeper than dark ink
pages turn in sync
permanent.

life changes, grows, and moves
but my kind of love for you
permanent.

The Little Things

. . .

it's the little things.

that sounded too simple before him.
"little things?" i thought
how can you have a grandiose, one for the ages love
with only little things?

i imagined being whisked away to Rome
painfully and helplessly inseparable
the kind of infatuation where you feel afloat . . .

i fantasized about gestures that were larger than life
a stereo on his shoulders outside of my window at night
running through the airport to stop me after a
     petty fight
climbing Mount Everest just to scream from the summit,
"this girl, she's mine."

it's none of that.

it's the coffee on my bedside table that's gone cold
    because he wakes hours before me, but leaves it
    there just in case.

it's the burnt pancakes three sundays in a row as he
    drowns the crisp edges in syrup pretending they
    are gourmet.

it's the stupid nicknames.
it's taking the dog for a walk.
it's picking between white or eggshell for the kitchen
    cabinets.
it's changing the oil.
it's holding hands across the center console.
it's listening to his guitar through the floorboards.
it's sitting in silence.
it's the fleeting, unconscious, innate moments.

it's the little things.

Moving Day

. . .

truck full of boxes
the garage door ascends
as one chapter closes
another begins

is it the death of my youth as i move to a house?
or the birth of my maturity finally coming around?

pink still splashes the walls
as a defiant pastel statement
my adolescence isn't going in
a box locked in the basement

there's still room for parties, a yard for a pool
i hope my friends still come over
i hope they still think i'm cool
when i mention that we left our penthouse view
for a house big enough for way more than two

i have to admit, hearing the birds in the morning
i thought would be loud, even downright annoying

but as i'm unpacking, arranging, and sorting
the birds in the backyard are a far cry from boring

and that extra room *will* be a beautiful nursery
even if it is a few years precursory
maybe that's not a bad thing to think about
maybe that was one of the reasons we moved out
and into this big white two-story house

truck full of boxes
the garage door ascends
as one chapter closes
another begins

Sunday Drive

. . .

there's something therapeutic about a Sunday drive
my husband has the wheel, i'm on the passenger side
soul-searching through the windshield and maybe even
    finding
a little peace of mind in these back roads unwinding

there are small houses fixed on their property grid
surrounded by cattle and horses, chickens and hens
i think about the endless hours the family must spend
with all that land and livestock to tend

we stumble upon antique shops
with trinkets stacked bottom to top
front windows littered with knickknacks begging to be
    dusted off
then collect more from new shelves they'll land atop

there's bluegrass playing
the windows are cracked
i'm not thinking, is my song on the other station
or what time to be back

my hair tousled from the breeze
his hand sits softly on my knee
we are heading nowhere, slowly
is this what it feels like to be free?

free from the weight that i place on my shoulders
and the "what-ifs" i spend hours mulling over
free from the opinions and the god-awful mentions
free from the filters and internet friendships

i wonder if we'll move out here one day
just a little bit farther away
yet a different world
less accessible to *what* i am,
and more to *who*
the roots of that girl

it's just a few miles out of town
it's just the road and the sky
it's just two hours and fifteen minutes
it's just a Sunday drive

Isn't It Sad

· · ·

isn't it sad when the sun goes down
the ease to see you slips away?
isn't it sad when the moon comes out
that we've lost another day?

isn't it sad we don't know how many
more days of light we have?
the thought of one without you lingers
and oh, isn't it sad.

V.

Growing

· · ·

age is just a number
but we spend most of our lives
wishing to accelerate it
or cut it off at the thighs.

i remember the mystery, the romance as a kid
thinking of leaving my youngness behind
imagining the ease, the attitude, the self-assuredness
that seems to only come with time.

first thirteen
teenagers could cuss and cruise and date
go to Sonic after Friday night football
and Panama City for spring break
texting crushes way past bedtime
faces covered in drugstore paint.

then sixteen
fast freedom
first taste of the real world
outside of hometown Edens

never going anywhere
dreaming of one day leaving.

then eighteen
practically grown up, right?
if i wanted a piercing or a tattoo
it was my waiver to sign
all choices would be my own
as i vote, or smoke Lucky Strikes.

then, of course, twenty-one
romanticizing a confetti-soaked floor
a blushed buzz from a cosmo
sangria on a summer porch
living story lines of party songs
dancing far from being a bore.

after that, my foot came off the gas
not hoping to stall
but not wanting to rush past
any more seconds i wouldn't get back.

"your twenties are the most fun"
they sell to us in magazines

so i want to be here, grounded
feeling everything.

now i'm inching towards thirty,
my friends and i seem worried
questioning if "they" were right
what if our best years *are* behind?

on girls' nights we reconsider a third glass of wine
because we know it will hurt in the morning.
five years ago that would have never crossed our minds
as we'd giggle and keep pouring.

we compare our preventative botox lines
talk shit on our partners' habits.
we spend our money on bridesmaids' dresses
vacation days and taxes.

we reminisce on Broadway nights
where we'd dance up by the dj
and wonder how we got away with so much
charm drunk leeway.

as i write this, it is my best friend's birthday
she has thirty candles on a gluten-free cake
while it approached, she called me crying
worried her youth had slipped away.

as her plea to stay young forever was explained
i listened, full well feeling just the same
but knowing that i had to say
something to ease the pain.

"you're not growing up,
you're just growing"
slipped from my eager-to-ease lips
and it's stuck with me ever since.

growing means we have been planted well
withstood storms and weathered hail
all these years being nurtured and watered
through every season, we haven't faltered.

our roots are deep and healthy and sturdy
enduring our patient parts being hurried
holding us down when winds of change fly
while letting us tiptoe our way to the sky.

so as we prune ourselves back
to preserve time from showing
we are not growing up,
we are just growing.

Not My Age

. . .

my daydreams still drift
to lands that don't exist
wild imagination creates
its own colors to paint
the scrunched-nosed
faces of constellations
a deep, velvet cobalt
a rich, dense slate

the ruffles my mother
once dressed me in
envelop my mind
reminding my
impatient nature
to slow its tread
to take its time

my hips are painted
in stripes
like a tiger
from growing up
too quick

back and legs ache from
growing pains you
only hope to
outgrow someday
but the tiger stripes,
those stay
i've grown to like
them anyway

i've been called
an old soul
before i knew
what a soul was
chubby cheeks
holding their place
to this day
insisting youth
still remains
life pinches them
taunting me

i'm a grown-ass woman
i'm a little girl

wise as an oak
naive as an unbroken heart

my spirit and being
are in charge
on different
days

my body and mind
never
reading
the same page

i wonder how old
i really am
certainly not
my age.

Music

. . .

you're my time machine home and my sweetest escape
ground me firmly and give me feathered wings
you're a loyal companion and a shadow i can't shake
ever-changing and all-consuming

you are coated in melodies and rolled in rhymes
stumbling to a poetic landing
you take over my mind
and use my hands for pen's sake,
we have that understanding

you know me better than i do, anyway

you have made me move rooms, houses, cities.
    mountains, too.
you've kept me wild, naive, silly.
absolute.
you've broken my heart, then given me the sounds to
    heal it

you're the rudest form of friendship i know.
you're the truest form of friendship i know.

i can't live without you
i resent the silence
i'd go deaf and i'd go mute
if you left me in the quiet

you are my truth, my guts, my legacy
unveiled and therapeutic
my greatest gift, my greatest strength.
my forever, my music

Nashville

. . .

this town tried to swallow me up
but its teeth weren't sharp enough

life had already trained
my skin to callus tough

back when i didn't make a penny
those around me
still made plenty

back when majors simply wouldn't
too young, too pop
too woman

it was all gasoline
on my wildfire
coughing up ashes
as melodies
covered in
smoky magic

doesn't it look glittery
from the outside?
my blessed, my lucky
doesn't disqualify
the shrapnel beating
up my pride
through every twist
of this ride
since i moved here
with my starry eyes
at fifteen

i love it here
i hate it here
they love me here
they hate me here
i wish they complimented
my songs
like they do
my legs

i will never leave
heart and fingers bleed

from wants, no, needs
to write, to sing

gatekeeper'd walls
so i learned to crawl
now my secret power
isn't the music at all

i just don't quit
elastic, resilient
i'll run the circles
till naysayers
go quiet

underdog syndrome
even when i win
trying to do right by
that head in clouds kid
who believed she could
and didn't stop till she did
and won't stop till she *does*

deep in my bones, it's meant to be
as i show up again, roll up my sleeves
i play hard, i play clean
ruthless for my dream

Flattered

. . .

those who seem to linger closely
but never ask your name
they already know it, studying your game.

don't waste your time in wonder
of why they won't befriend
just keep being the reason they can't put down the pen.

they'll emulate your being
but by then you'll have progressed
because while they're onto you, you're on to the next.

when they get close to summit
credit won't go where it's due
your ideas and influence will be introduced as new.

so all the passerbyers
that you think don't think you matter
are trailing one you've blazed
so while they imitate, be flattered.

Aesthetically Pleasing

. . .

if you only knew me from photos on the internet
you'd think my kitchen is clean, it'd seem my
    closets kept
rosy cheeks pillow lips sun-kissed strands of hair
a sunset and a first-class seat, off to anywhere

blue jeans with a label, the kind that hide my tummy
eating at nice restaurants, drink away my money
glowy summer skin, pricks of tiny needles
life of every party, terrified of people

dopamine runs low then top shelves look half empty
add another filter, make the gray scale seem more pretty
miss my mother's birthday on a boat in Santorini
edit inches off my figure then go flaunt in a bikini

spiting Peter Pans because i grew up too soon
hold my lover's hand in therapy for two
witnessing the world, homesick in my guts
sing loud for this town, but it's not "this town" enough

i'm here to remind you the other side of picket fences
it's not as picturesque as the modern day presents it
as our jealous eyes compare what's ours for perceiving
don't forget life isn't meant to be aesthetically pleasing

Put the Camera Down

. . .

there are certain things a photo cannot capture
the height of a mountain, the depth of its stature

the ocean as it kisses an infinity horizon
the waves keeping time of such a wondrous titan

the vastness of a desert, the dryness of her soul
the way the sand stacks high and the tumbleweeds roll

the sky at golden hour when the blue becomes
    undressed
then bronze and untamed yellows swallow up the rest

the way you look at me, right past armored skin
as the wild in your eyes whispers welcome in

there are certain things so magical, you want to keep
    around
but you'll only truly see it, if you put the camera down

Mother Earth

. . .

i've seen waves flirt in Byron and snow blanket Aspen
red and gold sunsets persuasive of magic
bird's-eyed Grand Canyons and dove waterfalls
wandered through woodlands, wild oaks rising tall

felt salt in your oceans heal from within
with a kiss from the sun that you welcome in
as the birds flutter high and the wildflowers bloom
then i rest in your grass as we laugh at the moon

should we all be so lucky to know you this well
with unfiltered stories of beauty to tell
of your splendor so pure and your being so giving
your resilience profound, and body forgiving

i hope we treat you better
give love that you deserve
start to return the favor
and mother Mother Earth.

Uncomfortably Alone

. . .

why are we so scared to be alone?
that question has been lingering over my head
since i was twenty years old.

is it because of our phones?
the quickness that we can feel love?
the gratification of a stranger's approval?
the ease of a little fake fun?

are we crippling the innate magic that can only be found
when we're left with our thoughts, no distractions
    around?

i write this uncomfortably alone in a cabin.
a retreat planned to do just this,
sit with myself and write down what happens.

the sky is purple. i'm about an hour from where
    i grew up.
the drive in reminded me of my hometown.

being here triggers the push and pull i still feel to it.
　with it.
a rhythm i usually busy myself to drown.

the air is cold and the smoke of a single cigarette lingers
　above me.
not much of a smoker, but stopped for gas on the
　drive up
and the tiny rebel within screamed
"who's going to stop you?"
i chuckled while asking for a pack of Camel Crush.

i wonder what else she has said over the years that
　i've missed
drenched in varying levels of companionship.

i listen to far too many crime podcasts to pretend that i
　will sleep tonight
so i am getting to know the way the wind brushes the
　tin roof
finding melodies in the sonics like it's singing for
　the moon.
there's a rustle in the fallen leaves as deer wander by.
it's subtle but charming, a soundtrack to my night.

this is about the time i'd be halfway through a cabernet,
blaring something mindless through a shitty speaker.
that's what my habits are telling me to do, but this isn't
    their trip.
they don't want to go deeper.

so, what if the ability to be alone is the very thing that
    makes us unique?
what if the only true and real way we *become*
    is to *be*?

if i can learn to not only tolerate but *enjoy* myself
laugh at my thoughts, sing for no one
ask questions of inner falsities until they come undone.
should we return to zero before we can truly go farther?
will i leave here a better wife? friend? daughter?

maybe we owe it to ourselves to get to know ourselves.

it's dark now and the chill in the air is sharp
i'm going to go cook myself a meal, strum on my guitar,
maybe read a book, stay off of my phone
and see what may happen
uncomfortably alone.

Learning to Love Me

. . .

morning arises as i greet my reflection
routinely in the bathroom mirror
but today, something is different
more welcomed, clearer

the sharpness usually staring back
is now a kind, warm expression
a look you give your closest friends
or use to dazzle first impressions

my eyes hold less judgment
and seemingly more color
have they always been so green?
i've never noticed, have others?

an effortless grin takes hold
of my still childlike cheeks
i watch as my face becomes
all dimples, lines, and teeth

i cautiously walk to my closet
slipping on a summer dress

i don't hate the way it hugs me
in fact, enjoy its cotton caress

speak out my affirmations and
for once start to believe them
not wanting to sprint out of my skin
just feeling bone-deep freedom

twenty-seven years of crawling
with my palms and knees all bloody
but today i stood, something's changed
i think i'm learning to love me

Showing Up

. . .

learning the art of just showing up is changing my
  life daily.

not a slouched-over, reeking of cheap tequila, barely
  functional type of showing up.

not a light is on but no one's home going through
  the motions
doing something but nothing type of showing up.

but being called unexpectedly, and uncomfortably
  saying "yeah, i'll be there."
doesn't mean you're ready, doesn't mean you aren't
  scared.
doesn't mean you won't suck or stumble or fail
but it means that you didn't tuck your tail.
it means that you chose the wonder of what could be
  over the comfort of your routine.
that you are open to the world and what it may or may
  not bring.

showing up with eagerness. with terrifying
    transparency.
with a foresight to know it could change your life
    substantially.
or not. and that's okay too.
because that isn't the part that's up to me or up to you.

just try it.
blindly and wildly agree when asked to do something
    you hadn't planned for.
when the hallway leads to an unmarked door
just tell your feet to pace the floor
until you've arrived.
you just may be surprised.

My Mother

. . .

if i could take back my teenage tune-outs, i would
the age where i wandered headfirst into womanhood
when my young forever ego listened to her least
i could have learned a thing or two, but i was too naive

zoned out while she reminisced about her glory days
the scholarship that let her leave that town and move
    away
running her own business twenty-something in LA
the time before my father when she almost got engaged

living in Hawaii, claiming it her great adventure
never really healing from that fallout with her sister
finding God then every Sunday singing I surrender
holding her head high regardless of the room she enters

i have pieces of her stories as if they were told in passing
but now as i've grown older, it's time that i start asking
the moments still unknown i hope to start unwrapping
filling in the gaps of years of memories i'm lacking

farthest from a stranger with so much to still discover
the hardest her heart broke, to her childhood favorite
    color
i know her best but nonetheless i can't help but wonder
what's still left to learn, as i get to know my mother.

Cheers

. . .

may our cups remain half full
and our hearts remain unbroken

may our glasses stay rose-colored
but opinions stay outspoken

may our feet be firmly planted
and our minds be full of wonder

may these be our greatest years
but our age be just a number

may this night be for the ages
while we're all right here together

may these drinks not drown our livers
and may this buzz last us forever

If You've Made It This Far

. . .

if you've made it this far
you know who i am
what makes me vibrant or gray

if you've made it this far
i've taken your hand
and told my soul that it's safe

if you've made it this far
i've spilled all my guts
uncovered twice-shy scars

if you've made it this far
and turn back around
you're leaving with my heart

More Than I Need

. . .

you will not get everything you want.
you will not get everything you deserve.
you will not get everything you work for.
you will not get everything you dream of.

but you will get what you are meant to have,
and that is worth so much more.

every time my hands feel empty,
they still hold more than i need.

A Rose

. . .

i pulled a thorn from my skin
peeved at the pain
searching for the garden
from where it came
finding nothing

by the time i bandaged my wound
i felt another sharply pierce
my side
my hip
my cheek
my thighs

a bloody mess of burgundy
blooming into a petaled dress
crying from the agony
encompassing me in a splintered hug
an embrace with no face
two arms of tough love

tainting the smoothness
i was once draped in

that made me easy to hold
and desirable naked
becoming stained in saturation
swallowed in perfume
but for the first time ever
starting to bloom

these thorns are now my
tailored clothes
new romance in my
roots below
a perfect mess
it took to grow
out of myself
and into a rose

Acknowledgments

I am deeply thankful and honored to have the people around me who brought this book to life—from those who inspired it, encouraged it, and printed the words on the paper you're now reading.

To my real life. My parents. My friends-turned-family. My exes. My heroes. My teenage years. My mistakes. My teammates. My body. My guitar. My house with a husband, a dog, and a yard. I feel like the luckiest girl in the world to have such a lived-in life to write about.

My managers Jason Owen and Lisa Ray, thank you for never looking at me like I've lost my mind when I tell you I want to try something outside of music. You don't bat an eye, only help find the most brilliant ways to allow me to evolve and experiment.

Cait Hoyt, our introductory phone call was explaining my first 10,000 words and asking if you thought anyone would want to publish a poetry book from a new-ish country singer. You laughed, and within weeks had the deal done with a dream team. You are a force, and I'm so grateful that you spearheaded this project with intention and excitement.

Mary Reynics and the entire Ballantine/Penguin Random House publishing group, thank you for being wonderful partners and believing in my storytelling. Mary, you pushed me to dive deeper and to edit smarter, a process that has made me fall even more in love with writing. You also were incredibly patient as I mulled over and repeatedly questioned or changed just about every single bit of this thing until the very last deadline. I'm truly honored to release my debut book alongside such incredible women.

KELSEA BALLERINI is an award-winning singer, songwriter, and producer. She made history as the only female country artist since Wynonna Judd to log three consecutive number one singles from a debut album. Ballerini has garnered two Grammy Award nominations, won two ACM Awards, and picked up the iHeartRadio Music Awards honor for Best New Country Artist in addition to other accolades. Thus far, she has achieved thirteen gold, platinum, and multiplatinum RIAA single and album certifications, six career number one singles on country radio, and global streams totaling more than three billion to date.

kelseaballerini.com

Twitter: @kelseaballerini

Instagram.com/kelseaballerini

Facebook.com/kelseaballerini

ABOUT THE TYPE

This book was set in Fournier, a typeface named for Pierre-Simon Fournier (1712–68), the youngest son of a French printing family. He started out engraving woodblocks and large capitals, then moved on to fonts of type. In 1736 he began his own foundry and made several important contributions in the field of type design; he is said to have cut 147 alphabets of his own creation. Fournier is probably best remembered as the designer of St. Augustine Ordinaire, a face that served as the model for the Monotype Corporation's Fournier, which was released in 1925.